Michael E. Degen has been teaching for the past twenty years at Jesuit College Preparatory School in Dallas, TX. He earned his B.A. at Loras College, his M.A. at the University of Dallas, his M.Ed. at the University of North Texas, and his Ph.D. at the University of Texas at Dallas.

Also by Michael E. Degen

Crafting Expository Argument: Practical Approaches to the Writing Process for Students and Teachers.

Prospero's Magic: Awaken Students' Critical Thinking Skills.

MICHAEL E. DEGEN

VIRGINIA WOOLF'S
A Room of One's Own

A CONTRIBUTION TO THE ESSAY GENRE

TELEMACHOS
PUBLISHING

Copyright 2014 by Michael E. Degen, Ph.D.
First edition

Telemachos Publishing
PO Box 460387
Garland, TX 75046-0387
www.telemachospublishing.com

Library of Congress Control Number: 2014934084
ISBN: 9780985384937

For Eileen Gregory, Ph.D.,

who graciously guided me through the beginning of my

graduate career, and who was kind enough to tell me that

my first draft of this essay needed a thorough revision.

Contents

Chapter One: Context 11

Chapter Two: Narration 29

Chapter Three: Description 41

Chapter Four: Exposition 53

Chapter Five: Persuasion 73

Chapter Six: Final Thoughts 79

Works Cited and Consulted 83

Acknowledgments 93

Chapter One
CONTEXT

If Virginia Woolf in *A Room of One's Own* "provided virtually every crucial metaphor [feminists] now use" as Patricia Joplin contends, and if she provided "a possible vision of what lay behind and beyond women's silence"(4), then, as Ellen Bayuk Rosenman says in the only book-length study of *A Room of One's Own*,

> Woolf's essay has become a canonical text for the
> multifaceted feminist literary criticism of the last two
> decades. *A Room of One's Own* is a primer of feminist
> concepts: the experience of oppression and victimization,
> the importance of exclusion and marginality, the existence of
> a distinctive female voice and subject matter. (13)

This critical assessment of Woolf's essay presents a significant problem. Predominately feminist readings of Woolf's essay have appropriated her work too narrowly; the voluminous appropriation suggests that the primary import of Woolf's essay is as a tract maligning male literary tradition. These critics, ironically, in seeking to elevate Woolf's essay, diminish and weaken it, implicitly suggesting that the essay cannot be seriously considered outside of a feminist context, that its contribution to a large and inclusive literary canon is, therefore, limited.

This critical appropriation of Woolf's essay is similar to the gender appropriation about which Woolf herself warns her audience in *A Room of One's Own*:

> "Female novelists should only aspire to excellence by courageously acknowledging the limitations of their sex." That puts the matter in a nutshell, and when I tell you, rather to your surprise, that this sentence was written not in August 1828 but in August 1928, you will agree, I think, that however delightful it is to us now, it represents a vast body of opinion. (75)

This contemporaneous criticism is only one instance in which Woolf makes the students at Newnham and Girton colleges aware of a "vast body of opinion" that represents a ridiculous reduction of women's capabilities. In an earlier section, for example, she briefly mentions "Mr. Justice [who] commented in the Divorce Courts upon the Shamelessness of Women"(33), and "Mr. Oscar Brown [who] was wont to declare 'that the impression left on his mind after looking over any set of examination papers, was that, irrespective of the marks he might give, the best woman was intellectually the inferior of the worst man'"(53).

In many ways, current feminist reflections on Woolf's essay commit a similar injustice. The discussion of *A Room of One's Own* must expand beyond the boundaries imposed upon it by *literati* who are feminists

first and then lovers of literature if Woolf's essay is to retain the
stature it deserves in the canon of English and modernist literature. A
discussion of Woolf's essay must begin examining, as Ellen Carol Jones
suggests, Woolf's form and style, one that "reflects and extends the
argument" in which "the meaning can be discovered in the presentation
itself" (235). This complex experimentation with presentation and its
relationship to meaning has largely been ignored in literary studies.

It is important, then, to engage this formal discussion of *A Room
of One's Own*, demonstrating that Woolf here contributes to the literary
tradition not mere feminist polemic, but sophisticated experimentation
and expansion of the essay form. This form, as Gyorgy Lukacs
recognizes in his 1910 book *Soul and Form*, "has not yet, today, traveled
the road to independence which its sister, poetry, covered long ago—
the road of development from a primitive, undifferentiated unity with
science, ethics and art" (13). As indicated in her many essays on the
genre and its exemplary devotees, the essay, for Woolf, ideally provides
the highest form of literary freedom, liberty unparalleled by that of
the novel, the poem, or the play. Moreover, Woolf's broad gestures of
creative freedom appear through her complex manipulation of rhetorical
modes, voice, and language. In one sense, these rhetorical strategies
become a metaphor for the limitless nature of the essay form and its
ability to imitate the freedom of the human imagination. A thorough
explanation of how Woolf achieves this liberty solidly places *A Room of*

One's Own among the century's finest imaginative achievements.

Some contemporary critics have indeed recognized that many readers have misread the essay, failing to see that the point is not the explicit feminist argument regarding 500 pounds and a room of one's own. Rosenman notes that *A Room of One's Own* "is one of the more misunderstood works of modern literature" (15), a work whose "tone and design... baffled its first reviewers" (15). Michael Rosenthal agrees, noting that the point of Woolf's essay is "the demonstration of ... a creative intelligence fashioning a work of art"(219), rather than the explicit proposition of 500 pounds and a room of one's own. And even Arnold Bennett, a contemporary of Woolf who stands as her literary antithesis, senses that the explicit thesis is not the issue: "Woolf's thesis is not apparently important to her, since she talks about everything but the thesis" (259). What Bennett does not consider, however, is that perhaps the explicit thesis is not the thesis at all.

Woolf frequently reflects on the nature of the essay, both its form and content, its purpose, its energy, its power. Her own reflections in many critical essays and reviews provide a context for reading *A Room of One's Own* as the product of her musings, emphasizing her acute self-consciousness concerning the genre. Woolf's extended reflections on the essay genre began as early as 1905 with "The Decay of Essay Writing" and continued throughout her career, her most elaborate discussions found in "Montaigne,"(1919) her most revered model; "The

Modern Essay"(1920); "Impassioned Prose" (1925); and "De Quincey's Autobiography" (1929). These are the essays in which Woolf espouses literary freedom in her own work and lauds such liberty in the work of others, writers who "puzzle the critics, who refuse to go in with the herd. They stand obstinately across the boundary lines, and do a greater service by enlarging and fertilising" ("Impassioned Prose" 362). This value of freedom is echoed by Elena Gualtieri, who, in a recent book-length discussion of Woolf's essays, contends that the essay form provides "the freedom ... for exploring and bringing to light what other genres cannot or do not want to expose" (50). Woolf's model for liberty is Montaigne, who, according to Woolf, "will act by his own light; by some internal balance will achieve that precarious and everchanging poise which, while it controls, in no way impedes the soul's freedom to explore and experiment" ("Montaigne" 75). For Woolf, Montaigne's essays capture the freedom of the soul that she, too, seeks.

> In these extraordinary volumes of short and broken, long and learned, logical and contradictory statements, we have heard the very pulse and rhythm of the soul, beating day after day, year after year, through a veil which, as time goes on, finds itself almost to transparency. (78)

In many ways, the reader of Woolf's essay feels, similarly, that he has viewed some of the complexity and mystery of her soul within a prose of contradictions and pulses and pauses.

Woolf's primary vehicle for experimentation occurs within the four modes of discourse—narration, description, exposition, and persuasion. She manipulates the modes to serve multiple rhetorical functions throughout the essay, often challenging the reader's traditional expectation for each mode, expanding its role. This creative gesture allows the reader to perceive from multiple angles. Woolf's fusion of modes has been noted by Gualtieri, who points out that "everywhere you look there is a cross-fertilization, overlap and the dissolving of divisions" (97). Moreover, using all four modes—at times independently and simultaneously—functions similarly to presenting multifarious voices; this multiplicity produces a rhapsody of form, each mode communicating with and engaging the reader, in a shared attempt to gain access to the complex and mysterious human soul.

The problem with most critical scholarship is its emphasis solely on Woolf's explicit surface content rather than on what occurs below this content—the experimentation in language and form. Woolf's content achieves value as its message is achieved in form. Much critical commentary explores how Woolf's essay delineates a variety of issues involving the female artist. One frequently discussed topic among scholars explores Woolf's implicit derision of patriarchy. In fact, Rosenman states that the essay "turns on two large, vague words: patriarchy and feminism" (30). Regarding feminism, Rosenman states that

> Woolf evolved a politics that insisted on several points: the
> importance of gender as a category in society, the fact of
> women's oppression, and the extent of women's abilities and
> values when left untrammeled by male domination.(34)

Others, like Julie Solomon, suggest that Woolf "advocates a tactic
of compliance with the existing power structure. She recommends
that women (like agile tightrope walkers) adapt themselves to the
'reality' of the dominant power structure through imitation of male
practice"(Solomon 340). Other critics of the essay explain the behavior
of patriarchy through a Freudian analysis of the male. For example,
in her discussion of the mirror image in Woolf's writing, Susan Squier
points out that "men need women to serve as magnifying mirrors in
order to fight off the continuing, debilitating suspicion that they are
never free of their primitive longing for that powerful mother figure"
(277).

Other feminist critics laud Woolf's essay as an explicit or implicit
challenge to the conventions of the literary world. Critics point to a
variety of rhetorical strategies Woolf employs to subvert tradition. For
instance, Jane Marcus and Jones recognize in Woolf's essay aspects
of classical rhetoric, her essay following the five-part sequence of
the *dispositio*—the *exordium, narratorio, confirmatio, refutatio,* and
peroration. These critics believe, as Marcus states, that Woolf "masters
the principles of classical rhetoric and subverts them at the same time"

("Taking the Bull" 148). When Woolf manipulates these rhetorical conventions in her "playful mocking" (Farrell 915), she attempts to "emancipate herself from the molds of conventional perception and language"(Jones 229). Another critic, Anne Fernald, believes that Woolf's essay contains "subversion and suggestion," devices "central to the rhetoric of personal criticism" (182). Lillian Bisson explains that the lecture form itself, and Woolf's use of it, "allows her to deliver a well-aimed blow at academic authoritarianism by subverting one of the mainstays of its power—the academic lecture" (202). Similarly, Dudley Marchi recognizes Woolf's use of "forms she learned from the male literary canon," forms, however, that then became "revitalized. . . in her own dynamic style" (2). Some critics, however, like Pamela Caughie, avoid labeling Woolf as subversive; rather, Caughie says, "the point of the essay is to introduce into the concept of tradition the concept of change, of instability" (45).

Though these feminist critics (Marcus, Fernald, others) seek to expand discussion of A Room of One's Own into issues of rhetoric and form, they do so only to amplify the feminist viewpoint; for them Woolf's use of rhetorical strategies deserves attention only to the extent that it undermines male literary tradition. For example, many critics discuss Woolf's use of the fictional narrator-personae. Marcus believes that Woolf creates a narrative synecdoche in which

she is not Virginia Woolf standing on the platform but the

> voice of the anonymous female victim of male violence
> throughout the ages. She transforms herself in the narrative to
> the object of her narration. (158)

In a similar manner, Jean Long notes that the narrative personae allow
Woolf to show "women who ... have reason to be angry, but never
actually are" (90). This, then, as Fernald writes, "inhibits us from
being distracted by Woolf the personality and allows us to enter into a
sympathetic relationship with the persona" (177). Caughie, however,
approaches the narrative differently, seeing Woolf's strategy as one
that "illuminate[s] her conception of the artist and the artwork" (40).
Moreover, Caughie states,

> the changeable "I" and flexible approach suggest that the
> truth we seek is not single but multiple, not subjective but
> intersubjective. What is "honest" about Woolf's method is its
> very self-consciousness. (43)

James Hoban writes, in "Rhetorical *Topoi in A Room of One's Own*,"
that Woolf's fictional narrator imitates a new "conception of invention"
(149). The narrator Mary Beton shows the reader, for example, how
one proceeds to invent topics, discovering ideas and formulating
techniques for presentation (Hoban 149). Hoban's discussion, though
appearing to examine Woolf's essay independently of feminist rhetoric,
however, does not stray far from the issues of politics and gender:

> Woolf's essay adds to a new view of rhetoric by eliminating

> anything that smacks of a system such as the rigid ordering
> of topics so prized by the ancients and their followers, and
> offering as an alternative an approach at once individualistic
> and suggestive, one appealing, at least initially, to the
> daughters of educated men. (151)

In addition to these considerations, Bisson explains that
Woolf's narrative helps her solve a contextual dilemma. Can Woolf
communicate her genuine feelings regarding patriarchal mistreatment
of women while she restrains a vitriolic anger? For, as Bisson
remarks, Woolf wishes to "preserve her own status in the male literary
establishment and ensure that her controversial message will receive a
more sympathetic hearing" (198). Bisson adds that

> her solution to the problem is found in the narrative stance of
> her persona. That persona ... is fluid, relational, fragmented—
> encompassing thousands of suppressed female voices. (198)

This "problem" of context that Bisson mentions—Woolf's oblique
strategy of addressing a male literary world—represents the topic of
additional criticism. Some critics, like Adrienne Rich, believe that
Woolf's essay is too accommodating to "male rhetoric," that the essay
acquiesces to the restrictions imposed by patriarchy. For Rich, Woolf's
resolution of her dilemma—as Alex Zwerdling defines it, "the conflict
between angry and conciliatory impulses" (246)—disappoints the
genuine feminist. In her essay "When We Dead Awaken: Writing as Re-

Vision," Rich laments what she sees as Woolf's restraint, her conciliatory and guarded tone.

> It is the tone of a woman almost in touch with her anger, who
> is determined not to appear angry, who is willing herself to
> be calm, detached, and even charming in a roomful of men
> where things have been said which are attacks on her very
> integrity .... Only at rare moments in that essay do you hear
> the passion in her voice. (Rich 37)

Rich, however, does not appear to consider that Woolf consciously and carefully chose a strategy in *A Room of One's Own*, chose to avoid explicit polemic, not out of fear but out of artistic preference. Woolf herself was aware of her dilemma. Writing in a letter to G.L. Dickinson, she admits, "My blood is apt to boil on this subject as yours does about natives, or war" (*Letters* IV 106). Moreover, Hoban counters Rich by noting that the reader of Woolf's essay is indeed "aware of Virginia Woolf's anger, her contempt for chauvinist men" (148). In addition, Zwerdling explains that Woolf did not avoid anger in her writing generally: "Anger is not consistently denied either in Woolf's feminist books or in her novels: it is frequently given its due" (251). Zwerdling believes that Woolf was readily aware of her anger but felt that placing

> those feelings on more prominent display would not, to her
> way of thinking, have produced better art... She felt that they
> were too unguarded, too artless. Anger could be the root but

must not be the flower. (252)

In fact, Woolf knew that her essay contained a subversive, subtle, and artful quality. In a letter to V.Sackville-West, she says, "Although you don't perceive it, there is much reflection and some erudition in it: the butterfly begins by being a loathsome legless grub" (101). Woolf's image of the "loathsome legless grub" may represent her raw anger in an artless, unbridled form.

A few critics attempt to move beyond these feminist readings and examine Woolf's rhetoric independent of political strictures. In particular, Thomas J. Farrell's examination of Woolf's essay reflects on its experimental quality. Though he uses gender terminology—labeling Woolf's use of male and female rhetoric—he does so to explore and expand the discussion of her essay beyond feminist ideology, believing that Woolf expands the essay form. Farrell explains that female rhetoric, on the one hand, is "open-ended...implicit and suggestive" (915), and it "seems to avoid unnecessary antagonism or differentiation," resulting in a mode that "appears to be more sincere, and especially in live deliberations, to be potentially (because less distracted by the contingencies of verbal combat) more centrally concerted than the male mode" (916). Male rhetoric, on the other hand, is more aggressive, combative, asserting its thesis immediately and proceeding to delineate its points in a logical fashion, believing that "it is impossible to win over the whole audience, so why try" (916). Farrell sees Woolf's essay as a blending of these two rhetorics; moreover, he says,

> It is possible to blend the best features of the two modes of
> rhetoric, but to do so requires even more conscious control
> than what either mode in itself requires, for blending the best
> features necessitates consciously and knowingly choosing those
> features and then using them effectively. *A Room of One's Own*
> is an instance of such blending. (921)

Whereas Farrell seeks to use rhetoric to explore what he senses is
experimentation with the essay form, Ellen Rogat's examination of
rhetoric returns to a feminist appropriation of Woolf's essay. While
rhetoric is Rogat's topic, it serves to emphasize what she sees as Woolf's
aggressive attack on the male world: Woolf "undercuts the tone of
certainty which pervades the masculine sentence" (88) because "she does
not want [readers] to think of her as a rigid presence, asserting her ego
and controlling their responses" (88), a characteristic more typical of
male rhetoric. These critics refer to these nuanced distinctions between
male and female rhetoric—what Marcus calls Woolf's "invention of
a female language" ("Sapphistry" 187)—as a method Woolf uses to
challenge literary tradition.

This issue of male and female rhetoric even appeared in early
reviews of *A Room of One's Own*. For example, an early 1929 unsigned
review from the *Times Literary Supplement* recognizes in *A Room of
One's Own* a male rhetoric: "It is certainly of interest to find an artist

who has (one is tempted to say) so masculine a sense of literary form as Mrs. Woolf" (*Times Literary Supplement* 256). In another review, V.Sackville-West sees the essay as a successful blending of the masculine and the feminine, her comments anticipating those of Farrell: "You might forget that her extravagances, if they have imagination and poetry for grandparents on the maternal side, have also sense and erudition for grandparents on the paternal" (257). Finally, Bennett, the misogynist whose book *Our Woman* claims that women are naturally inferior to men, reviewed *A Room of One's Own* in the Evening Standard (1929), noting the "feminine" associational quality of the essay:

> If I had to make one of those brilliant generalisations now so fashionable, defining the difference between men and women, I should say that whereas a woman cannot walk through a meadow in June without wandering all over the place to pick attractive blossoms, a man can. Virginia Woolf cannot resist the floral enticement. (259)

Though Bennett's comments here demonstrate explicitly a criticism shallow and misogynistic, he nonetheless reflects the initial reaction that Woolf's rhetoric moves beyond traditional boundaries of exposition. Unfortunately, current criticism has not moved much past Bennet's initial recognition of Woolf's experimentation with the essay genre; in ignoring Woolf's numerous written reflections on the essay and merely reading *A Room of One's Own* within a political context, scholars denigrate her contribution to the literary world. While neither Woolf herself nor A Room of One's Own avoids feminist issues, current scholarship has failed to discuss adequately Woolf's tremendous contribution to genre theory.

Chapter Two
NARRATION

The reader first recognizes traditional boundaries broadened through Woolf's use of the narrative mode—initially functioning as an apt approach to arrangement—the *dispositio*. Woolf's narrative relies primarily on a fictional personae; the character Mary Beton is at first imagined as "sitting on the banks of a river a week or two ago in fine October weather, lost in thought"(5). Here, narrative has various uses. First, it introduces the archetype of the quest, the journey; specifically, within this context, the essay form represents a journey, a recursive process in which one frequently stops, pauses, redirects, and redefines, rather than a process in which one easily moves forward in a linear manner. Though this type of journey may prove frustrating, Woolf suggests that it finally produces a greater intellectual insight than a linear development. Woolf explicitly speaks of this process, insisting that "we should start without any fixed idea where we are going to spend the night, or when we propose to come back; the journey is everything" ("Montaigne" 76). Lukacs, too, discusses the searching nature of the essay, explaining that the essay form imitates the longing of the human soul for consummation, "an original and deep-rooted attitude towards the whole of life, a final, irreducible category of possibilities of experience"(17).

Woolf's recursive narrative imitates this desire to explore life's possibilities. She first finds her placid journey to the library interrupted by a beadle, whose face "expressed horror and indignation"(6) at her trespassing on the lawn. Once this crisis ends, she continues excitedly toward the library to read Lamb's essay on "Lycidas." Her plan to proceed is then thwarted by the "kindly gentleman" who forbids her entry into "the door which leads into the library"(7). Despite her redirection of energy, she nonetheless moves forward and later engages in reflection—"I pondered this and that, as one does at the end of the day's work" (24). The reflective gesture here captures the nature of the essay, its ability to allow one to be thinking, be considering always "the whole thing more carefully before [one goes] any further"(91). Here is Woolf's initial vision of the flexibility of the essay form, one that allows an artist's mind to alter direction, to engage, to be alert, to be prepared. In "The Modern Essay," Woolf asserts that the essayist should "sting us wide awake and fix us in a trance which is not sleep but rather an intensification of life—a basking, with every faculty alert. ..."(216). Woolf's narrative experimentation does keep her reader wide awake and its placement so early in her essay indicates that her prominent concern is that of form and its possibilities for meaning, rather than that of content and depiction of a vituperative feminist voice.

The narrative journey often transports one to unexpected locations, which stimulate additional thoughts, offering ways to weave new ideas into the writer's argument. Woolf admires this aspect of DeQuincey, "a reflective writer, who with only prose at his command ... made his way into precincts which are terribly difficult of approach" ("Impassioned Prose" 367). Woolf explores such precincts, for example, while eating lunch after her British Museum visit. Woolf is "interrupted by the necessity of paying the bill. It came to five shillings and ninepence. I gave the waiter a ten-shilling note and he went to bring me change"(37). This narrative interruption provides an opportunity for additional expository commentary, as she observes "another ten-shilling note in my purse; I noticed it, because it is a fact that still takes my breath away— the power of my purse to breed ten-shilling notes automatically" (37). This interruption, then, has not been a futile distraction, but another opportunity to reinforce her explicit argument regarding the necessity of money for intellectual freedom. Fernald recognizes that "interruption is both a method and a theme" (178), explaining that these interruptions

> acknowledge the readers' own interrupted reading, and
> reward our efforts to follow her argument with a change
> of perspective, ... a comic reminder of the impossibility of
> coming to a conclusion. (178)

To be comfortable with a lack of conclusion and even contradiction, accepting a sort of negative capability, is a quality to be admired in an artist, as John Burt points out (193). Woolf, too, admits that she does not fear contradiction; for her, this quality of the essay provides a freedom from appropriation.

> Movement and change are the essence of our being; rigidity
> is death; conformity is death: let us say what comes into our
> heads, repeat ourselves, contradict ourselves, fling out the
> wildest nonsense, and follow the most fantastic fancies without
> caring what the world does or thinks or says. For nothing
> matters except life; and, of course, order. (75)

Woolf here, though, is careful not to confuse freedom with chaos, which
does not enhance liberty but restricts it, a chaos produced by unbridled
passion. In addition, Woolf's narrative posits more than mere content;
it shows the reader the process, the journey toward uncovering truth,
a task equally important as the assertion of content. For instance,
while Woolf's content explores the more explicit theme of the female
artist and economics, which could easily be accomplished with
straightforward exposition, the narrative extends itself by demonstrating
to the reader how the writer arrived at the conclusion, modeling and
imitating an intellectual gesture, and creating a subtle didacticism, all
contributing to the intimacy between writer and reader.

The narrative structure also allows the writer to persuade
implicitly—and, thus, more effectively—by eschewing tones of
anger, bitterness, or confrontation. In this way, narrative provides
an emotional distance that mitigates what possibly may offend one's
audience. As a result, Zwerdling proposes, the reader finds that in
Woolf's essay,

> in place of anger we have irony; in place of sarcasm, charm.
> The choices are designed not only to win over the opposition
> but also to reinforce the image of the author's cool self-
> possession. Her technique is both concessive and seductive.
> (255)

For example, within her narration of confronting the beadle on
the lawn, she implicitly provides details concerning the current
discrimination against women rather than explicitly writing declarative
expository, the former a rhetorical choice that allows one's audience to
feel more at ease with topics otherwise controversial. Woolf writes of
this technique in her essay "Mr. Bennett and Mrs. Brown." There she
declares the writer must get into touch with his reader by putting

> before him something which he recognizes, which therefore
> stimulates his imagination, and makes him willing to co-
> operate in the far more difficult business of intimacy. And it
> is of the highest importance that this common meeting-place
> should be reached easily, almost instinctively, in the dark, with
> one's eyes shut. (111)

Her narrative continues to develop this implicit argument when,
opening the library door, she meets a "kindly gentleman, who regretted
in a low voice as he waved me back that ladies are only admitted to the
library if accompanied by a Fellow of the College or furnished with

a letter of introduction"(7-8). Here she subtly describes the obstacles the contemporary woman must still face, introducing this material with rhetorical aplomb. Her use of the narrative mode demonstrates not only the possibilities of the mode itself but also the flexibility and cleverness of the essay form, a vehicle of tremendous freedom. Certainly, the traditional essay form reliant solely on exposition could not accommodate this level of liberty.

Narration also provides opportunity to create persuasive analogues, using concrete events and images, in this context, to speak to the condition of the female artist. Again, in the opening scene with the beadle, Woolf explains that she starts moving toward the library because of her excitement over the "tumult of ideas," which made it "impossible to sit still" (6). She then writes that "instantly a man's figure rose to intercept me" (6). Within this apparently innocent and banal narrative resides an analogue—that women's intellectual efforts and desires are constantly thwarted by patriarchy, that these forces frequently appear to set boundaries for the female artist. Once again, the analogue is less demonstrative than stating, for instance, that men frequently thwart the creative efforts of women. In fact, the subtlety of the narrative analogue imitates the sometimes insidious subtlety of discrimination. As Woolf explains, "For one does not say everything; there are some things which at present it is advisable only to hint" ("Montaigne" 75). Moroever, Woolf's stylistic adroitness communicates to her audience an important lesson: "One place that the patriarchy does not dominate is her imagination" (Hoban 153). And it is the essay form that provides so many options for the imagination to exercise its liberty.

Narration also contributes to the emotional appeal (pathos) of her explicit argument, one of the three appeals of persuasion that Aristotle groups under "artistic" proof (Corbett and Connors 18). This emotional appeal again occurs quite subtly in the narrative as Mary Benton departs from Oxbridge and walks through the avenue: "Gate after gate seemed to close with gentle finality behind me" (13). Hidden within this narration is the image of barriers that still exist for women. A more overtly emotional narrative occurs during her episode regarding Judith Shakespeare. The imagined scenario demonstrates the injustices women face and the price society pays for their continued perpetuation of crimes against women. Woolf explains that Judith Shakespeare

> picked up a book now and then, one of her brother's perhaps, and read a few pages. But then her parents came in and told her to mend the stockings or mind the stew and not moon about with books and papers…. Soon, however, before she was out of her teens, she was to be betrothed to the son of a neighboring wool-stapler. She cried out that marriage was hateful to her, and for that she was severely beaten by her father. Then he ceased to scold her. He begged her instead not to hurt him, not to shame him in this matter of her

marriage.... she made up a small parcel of her belongings, let
herself down by a rope one summer's night and took the road
to London.... Nick Greene the actor-manager took pity on her;
she found herself with child by that gentleman and so—who
shall measure the heat and violence of the poet's heart when
caught and tangled in a woman's body?–killed herself one
winter's night and lies buried at some cross-roads where the
omnibuses now stop outside the Elephant and Castle. (47–48)

Here narrative allows Woolf to distance herself from an explicit
argument that could more forcefully delineate the unfairness and
damage done to women who challenge cultural gender roles. Her
narrative makes several points important for her case concerning the
intellectual freedom of women: one, women have been considered
property; two, males have been sly and deceitful; and three, women
have had few choices—subservience, poverty, or death. In addition,
Woolf's narration implicitly asks the audience to consider how much
and to what degree society has changed from the world of Judith
Shakespeare. Moreover, in this narrative, Woolf seeks "to communicate
a soul. . . . to go down boldly and bring to light those hidden thoughts
which are the most diseased; to conceal nothing; to pretend nothing"
("Montaigne" 76). And though Woolf's narrative content possesses
passion, its narrative structure possesses control, for Woolf knows that

Bad books are written in a state of boiling passion, with a complete certainty of inspiration. The bad books are not the mirrors but the vast distorted shadows of life; they are a refuge, a form of revenge. ("Bad Writers" 328)

Narrative allows Woolf to avoid the chaos of revenge, to escape the danger of passion restricting liberty.

Chapter Three
DESCRIPTION

Within this narration, Woolf expands the nature of the essay form through her skill with description, her writer's eye and ear. In a letter to Stephen Spender, 10 July 1934, Woolf expresses her awareness of the power and freedom of description:

"I should like to write four lines at a time, describing the same feeling, as a musician does; because it always seems to me that things are going on at so many different levels simultaneously" (352). Once again, multiplicity for Woolf results in greater liberty of expression. First, her description relies on the power of poetic language—extended metaphor, even conceit, as well as personification and alliteration. Her ability to control language, to use language to communicate a vision, contributes to her ethos as writer. Language expands one's liberty, as Mario Vargas Llosa notes recently in an article in *The New Republic*, commenting that

> to have at one's disposal a rich and diverse language, to be able to find the appropriate expression for every idea and every emotion that we want to communicate, is to be better prepared to think, to teach, to learn, to converse, and also to fantasize, to dream, to feel.... And as language evolved...and reached high levels of refinement and manners, it increased the possibility of human enjoyment. (33)

Woolf's poetic descriptions demand a more complete engagement from the reader. In her essay "How One Should Read a Book?" Woolf discusses how "metaphors are then more expressive than plain statements," and require the reader "to use all our energies of mind to grasp the relation between" (395). This communal aspect of the essay provides an opportunity for experimentation not only by the writer but the reader as well. "A writer is never alone," Woolf reminds us. "There is always the public with him—if not on the same seat, at least in the compartment next door" ("Mr. Bennett and Mrs. Brown" 113). If the reader is then a participant, the essay form itself has engaged its audience to a greater degree than the other genres, establishing an ownership that lends to the essay's persuasive effect, its ability to change the reader's perception. For example, within the first few pages of *A Room of One's Own*, Woolf creates an elaborate conceit—comparing fishing to thinking.

> Thought—to call it by a prouder name than it deserved—had let its line down into the stream. It swayed, minute after minute, hither and thither among the reflections and the weeds, letting the water lift it and sink it, until—you know the little tug—the sudden conglomeration of an idea at the end of one's line: and then the cautious hauling of it in, and the careful laying of it out? Alas, laid on the grass how small, how insignificant this thought of mine looked; the sort of

> fish that a good fisherman puts back into the water so that it
> may grow fatter and be one day worth cooking and eating....
> But however small it was, it had, nevertheless, the mysterious
> property of its kind—put back into the mind, it became at
> once very exciting, and important; and as it darted and sank,
> and flashed hither and thither, set up such a wash and tumult
> of ideas that it was impossible to sit still. (5-6)

That Woolf opens her essay with such a controlled and elaborate
metaphorical exercise suggests that her primary interest in this essay is
experimentation with form rather than experimentation with political
rhetoric. For instance, the conceit imitates the pulse and rhythm
present in the essay form, its resistance to appropriation—"it swayed . . .
hither and thither among reflections and the weeds." In this movement,
the essay at times submits to forces outside itself—"letting the water lift
it and sink it," but submission does not diminish its power; it merely
enhances it as the reader next encounters "the sudden conglomeration
of an idea" and "a wash and tumult of ideas." In addition, the
conceit speaks to the discovery aspect of the essay form, that however
"insignificant this thought of mine looked," it can possess a "mysterious
property." Finally, the early placement of the conceit presents a
disciplined mind, controlled and sustained in its reflection. Ironically,
this control appears to contradict the apparent randomness of the essay's
content. But Woolf has thus achieved what she felt Mr. Simon achieved

in his work: "These papers are for the most part short: but they are aimed directly at the heart of the subject that in each case they seem to show us something we had missed before" ("Mr Symon's Essays" 67).

Woolf's frequent and skilled use of rhetorical schemes also enhances her poetic prose. Woolf believes "the best prose is that which is most full of poetry" ("Montaigne" 74). In fact, James Naremore says that Woolf "claimed to be ignorant of metrics, yet her prose style is distinguished by its love of hypnotic rhythms"(17). Moreover, Naremore adds, "One has the sense that rhythm is what Virginia Woolf feels most of all when she writes; it is the thing that guides her pen" (18). Once again, rhetorical schemes demand control and concentration from the writer, a balance that restrains sometimes volatile content. For example, one notes her use of isocolon, a parallelism that balances units of identical word length and even syllable count: "the cautious hauling of it in, and the careful laying of it out?"(5). Other examples of parallelism occur frequently throughout this passage: "It swayed, minute after minute, hither and thither among the reflections and the weeds"(5). In addition, Woolf adds alliteration to the prose: "letting the water lift it and sink it, until—you know the little tug"(5). This same line even contains assonance, the repetition of the "i" sound: "It swayed, minute after minute, hither and thither. . . letting the water lift it and sink it, until—you know the little tug"(5). This sound creates a mood of anticipation or exasperation; punctuation also helps develop this mood—the commas, the dash, the semicolon—all working to extend the sentence, stretching it out as if to mimic the methodical process of reeling in one's line, waiting until the hook finally breaks the surface of the water, revealing one's prize. Woolf's poetic expression here fulfills her own definition of "a good essay," which "must draw its curtain round us, but it must be a curtain that shuts us in, not out" ("The Modern Essay" 224). Once inside this curtain, the writer and reader both have time to explore and to uncover the pulse and detail of the human soul.

The artist's descriptive power contributes to argument, too, specifically the *narratio*, that part of the argument in which one establishes the current situation, in this case, the continued economic disparity of women. Using description for persuasive purposes clearly expands the traditional expository essay form, providing the writer with additional options for persuading its reader. The clearest example occurs in the opening chapter in which Woolf juxtaposes two meals—one at Oxbridge and the other at Fernham. The montage effect forcefully points to the economic privilege of men over women. At Oxbridge

> ...the college cook had spread a counterpane of the whitest cream, ... After that came the partridges, but if this suggests a couple of bald, brown birds on a plate you are mistaken. The partridges, many and various, came with all their retinue of sauces and salads, the sharp and the sweet, each in its order; their potatoes, thin as coins but not so hard; their sprouts,

> foliated as rosebuds but more succulent.... Meanwhile the
> wineglasses had flushed yellow and flushed crimson; had been
> emptied; had been filled. (10-11)

Woolf follows, a few pages later, with description of her meal at
Fernham, a meal described with sentences that start and stop abruptly,
imitating her own amazement at the poverty of the feast and imitating
the difficulty in describing the meal; the sentences almost appear unable
to move forward.

> Here was the soup. Dinner was being served in the great
> dining-hall. Far from being spring it was in fact an evening in
> October. Everybody was assembled in the big dining-room.
> Dinner was ready. Here was the soup. It was a plain gravy
> soup. (17)

Even the redundancy of detail imitates the writer's bewilderment at the
scarcity of the surrounding meal. Eventually, though, Woolf musters
some elaboration for an uninspiring meal.

> One could have seen through the transparent liquid...next
> came beef with its attendant greens and potatoes—a homely
> trinity, suggesting the rumps of cattle in a muddy market, and
> sprouts curled and yellowed at the edge.... Biscuits and cheese
> came next, and here the water-jug was liberally passed round,
> for it is the nature of biscuits to be dry, and these were biscuits

to the core. That was all. The meal was over. (17-18)

Much like narration, description mutes the more aggressive and confrontational voice of persuasion, but still transmits the writer's voice. This muting enhances the effectiveness of the essay form in that it reaches a wider audience, again metaphorically resisting appropriation, enhancing freedom.

Finally, description, like narrative, can establish intellectual analogues, analogues produced by close meditation on the concrete world, leading to an opportunity of greater insight into the truth of the human condition. Woolf explicitly recognizes the presence of meaning in the insignificant. She explains that "the writer, as I think, has the chance to live more than other people in the presence of this reality. It is his business to find it and collect it and communicate it to the rest of us" (110). Woolf demonstrates this lesson toward the end of her essay, where in describing a leaf's movement, she presents an analogue for the act of intellectual reflection and for the nature of the essay form itself. This passage illustrates what Laura Marcus identifies as Woolf's strategy of examining details closely so that she can "transmit that emotion, very often by lingering on the atmosphere of a particular scene" (100).

> A single leaf detached itself from the plane tree at the end of
> the street, and in that pause and suspension fell. Somehow it
> was like a signal falling, a signal pointing to a force in things

which one had overlooked. It seemed to point to a river, which flowed past, invisibly, round the corner, down the street, and took people and eddied them along, as the stream at Oxbridge had taken the undergraduate in his boat and the dead leaves. Now it was bringing from one side of the street to the other diagonally a girl in patent leather boots, and then a young man in a maroon overcoat; it was also bringing a taxicab; and it brought all three together at a point directly beneath my window; where the taxi stopped; and the girl and the young man stopped; and they got into the taxi; and then the cab glided off as if it were swept on by the current elsewhere. (96)

This description, similar to Woolf's fishing conceit, speaks to the pulse of the essay form, its nature to be "a signal point to a force in things which one had overlooked." The essay, in addition, is a force that connects disparate things and images "ordinary enough" (96)—"it was bringing from one side of the street to the other diagonally a girl...." And finally, those parts the essay discovers can be brought into a larger whole, as she describes the eventual path of the single leaf which "brought all three together." In this moment, the essay has achieved wholeness: "Unity had been restored by seeing two people come together and get into a taxi-cab...for certainly when I saw the couple get into the taxi-cab the mind felt as if, after being divided, it had come together again in a natural fusion"(97-98). Woolf's description of the leaf demonstrates, too, how this mode can take an abstract idea—the nature of the essay form—and make it concrete for the reader. Woolf believes that concrete description can also lead to greater freedom. In her essay "Mr. Bennet and Mrs. Brown," Woolf urges writers to "describe beautifully if possible, truthfully at any rate, our Mrs. Brown. You should insist that she is an old lady of unlimited capacity and infinite variety; capable of appearing in any place; wearing any dress; saying anything and doing heaven knows what" (119). Here, Mrs. Brown is the emblem for the unrestrictive potential in description, its ability to escape time and place.

Chapter Four
EXPOSITION

Traditional essay form relies predominately on ordered and systematic exposition. Woolf does not exclude this mode, but demonstrates how this traditional mode, too, can provide numerous options for the essayist. Exposition more explicitly contributes to her ethical appeal (*ethos*) by displaying her skill with rhetorical schemes, and by crafting a variety of sophisticated voices. First, her exposition, in allowing her to create an ethical appeal (*ethos*), demonstrates that she possesses *phronesis* (sound of sense), *arete* (high moral character), and *eunoia* (benevolence) (Corbett 45). Woolf establishes early in her essay her literary sense—a comprehensive education and an ability to read well. For example, in her brief comments regarding Charles Lamb, she explains Lamb's essays as acts of "wild flash of imagination, that lightning crack of genius in the middle of them which leaves them flawed and imperfect, but starred with poetry" (7). Later, she catalogues for her audience her familiarity with some of the great works of literature, explaining how

> women have burnt like beacons in all the works of all the
> poets from the beginning of time—Clytemnestra, Antigone,
> Cleopatra, Lady Macbeth, Phedre, Cressida, Rosalind,
> Desdemona, the Duchess of Malfi, among the dramatists; then
> among the prose writers: Millamant, Clarissa, Becky Sharp,

Anna Karenina, Emma Bovary, Madame de Guermantes. (43)

The effect of this cataloguing and the lists that appear, for example, while she is in the British Museum, may at first seem superfluous, though contributing to the audience's perception of Woolf as an educated and perspicacious artist. She is not merely listing names, but taking in a variety of detail; her cataloguing is an image of the limitless possibility of exposition.

These examples lead to her more extended expository analysis of the paucity of female writers over the past few centuries, beginning with the sixteenth century. Again, her objective goes beyond cataloguing; rather, she demonstrates her ability to analyze literary texts. Caughie explains in particular that Woolf delineates several intellectual approaches: "introspection (chap.2), historical reconstruction (chap.3), literary history (chap.4), textual analysis (chap.5)" (41). For example, she introduces Lady Winchilsea, born in 1661, beset by an "indignation against the position of women," her mind "harassed and distracted with hates and grievances" (59). Woolf does not merely assert these positions, she supports her stance with text from Winchilsea's poetry. In her analysis, Woolf recognizes what restricts Winchilsea's creative liberty: "Yet it is clear that could she have freed her mind from hate and fear and not heaped it with bitterness and resentment, the fire was hot within her" (60). When Winchilsea is able to restrain her anger, Woolf recognizes, this disgruntled writer produces "words of pure poetry:

"*Nor will in fading silks compose, / Faintly the inimitable rose*"(61). She then turns to Margaret of Newcastle, followed by Mrs. Behn, who, the author points out, "was a middle-class woman with the plebeian virtues of humour, vitality and courage; a woman forced by the death of her husband and some unfortunate adventures of her own to make her living by her wits"(64). This entire section communicates to her audience that she has researched and reflected cogently on the topic for which she speaks. But this exploration of detail regarding the limited canon of female artists illustrates Woolf's belief that "No fact is too little to let it slip through one's fingers, and besides the interest of facts themselves, there is the strange power we have of changing facts by the force of the imagination" ("Montaigne" 78).

Two additional points might be mentioned regarding Woolf's exposition. One is that this mode occurs primarily in the middle of the essay, illustrating Woolf's interest in first preparing the reader for difficult content by delaying it until one's reader is on more stable ground. Two, her extended discussion of these early female writers suggests Woolf's focus beyond political polemic and more toward literary expression and possibility, identifying potential and liberty lost.

Within the expository mode, Woolf provides order and balance through her use of a variety of rhetorical schemes. In fact, as her exposition becomes more explicitly political, the need is greater to shape and restrain potential anger. Lukacs makes a similar point about the challenge of style within the essay. He writes of "the universal problem of style: to achieve equilibrium in a welter of disparate things, richness and articulation in a mass of uniform matter" (6). Woolf achieves balance through the great variety of schemes, the tools of restraint. In addition, one sees Woolf's use of a variety of schemes as an analogue for the mutlifarious paths by which the essay approaches a topic, again speaking to the flexibility of the essay form. Woolf, too, speaks of the importance of style and its relationship to content in a letter to Janet Case, 1 September 1925: " The better a thing is expressed, the more completely it is thought. To me, [Robert Louis] Stevenson is a poor writer, because his thought is poor, and therefore, fidget though he may, his style is obnoxious. And I don't see how you can enjoy technique apart from the matter" (Banks 197). Casey Miller and Kate Swift, in *Words and Women*, note that without a level of stylistic sophistication, a writer's "language limits the thinking of its speakers to ideas they can express in that language" (137).

In addition to the previously discussed schemes, Woolf frequently employs anaphora, anastrophe, andiplosis, asyndeton, polsyndeton, parenthesis, and parallelism.

> ...the sketch of the angry professor had been made in anger. Anger had snatch my pencil while I dreamt. (31) [*anadiplosis*: repeating the last word of one clause at the beginning of the following clause]

He was the proprietor of the paper and its editor and sub-editor. He was the Foreign Secretary and the Judge. He was the cricketer; he owned the race-horses and the yachts. He was the director of the company.(33) [*anaphora*: repeating the same word or groups of words at the beginning of clauses]

...he it is who will acquit or convict the murderer.... (34) [anastrophe: inverting syntax]

It was distressing, it was bewildering, it was humiliating. (30) [*asyndeton*: omission of conjunctions]

Very soon he got work in the theatre, became a successful actor, and lived at the hub of the universe, meeting everybody, knowing everybody, practicing his art on the boards, exercising his wits in the streets, and even getting access to the palace of the queen. (47) [*parallelism*]

For truth...those dots mark the spot where, in search of truth, I missed the turning up to Fernham. (15) [*parenthesis*: an interruption in syntax]

It is part of the novelist's convention not to mention soup and salmon and ducklings, as if soup and salmon and ducklings were of no importance. (10) [*polysyndeton*: use of multiple conjunctions]

Woolf's creative play with syntax provides another emblem for the essay's expansive liberty. This varied syntax accomodates complex ideas, a quality she admires in DeQuincey and demonstrates herself:

> Then followed a discipline exacted...the weighing of cadences, the consideration of pauses; the effect of repetitions and consonances and assonances—all this was part of the duty of a writer who wishes to put a complex meaning fully and completely before his reader. (144)

Variety allows Woolf to avoid what she has said "is as a plague of locusts—the voice of a man stumbling drowsily among loose words, clutching aimlessly at vague ideas. . . " ("The Modern Essay" 217). Once again, Woolf recognizes that, paradoxically, a style controlled is a necessary element of liberty: "This freedom, then, which is the essence of our being, has to be controlled" ("Montaigne 75). In fact, though Jones speaks specifically about rhetorical style, her comments can be applied to the nature of the essay form itself:

> To attain the freedom and fullness of expression which are of the essence of art, both language and style must stretch, expand, transcend their present use if they are to portray adequately the experience of women. (234)

Of course, for Woolf, the use of schemes alone is not enough, for to be too "preoccupied with the effort to be smooth, rotund, demure, and irreproachable, sentimentality slips past unnoticed, and platitudes spread themselves abroad with an air of impeccable virtue" ("Imitative Essays" 249).

Not only do Woolf's rhetorical schemes reflect the layered complexity of the essay form, but her variety of voices also contributes to the resistance against appropriation. Woolf's voices satisfy her desire to use a form that "will include all the varieties of thought which are suitably enshrined in essays" ("The Decay of Essay Writing" 25). Several critics have commented on the voices in Woolf's essays, most critics drawing the reader's attention to the variety of voices as a result of the changing narrative personae (Mary Beton, Mary Seton, etc.) or voices referred to and quoted (Judith Shakespeare, Charlotte Bronte, Lady Winchilsea, etc.). Unfortunately, too many critical discussions of voice straitjacket the essay into a feminist context. Jean Long believes that Woolf's other female voices express the author's anger "ventriloquially" (90). Zwerdling makes a similar observation, noting that these additional voices are incorporated into Woolf's text as a means of simultaneously voicing injustice while removing herself from vitriolic polemic (253). In addition, Lauren Rusk adds that "insisting that she as speaker might have any woman's name, Woolf refuses to identify her experience as singular" (4).

Critics have failed to notice, however, that within Woolf's primary narrative voice itself (referred to as Mary Beton, Mary Seton, etc.) she creates a polyphony of modulated voices, which prevents the reader from assigning Mary Beton, for example, as merely one dimensional—for she can be academic, demure, and humorous. Woolf's use of these modulated voices within the dominant narrative personae creates additional layers of complexity, expanding her creative liberty; the variety of voices of each narrative personae escape appropriation and express a complexity that enhances the writer's ethos. Voice allows Woolf to use "every one of the senses [Nature] has given us; vary our state as much as possible; turn now this side, now that, to the warmth, and relish to the full before the sun goes..." ("Montaigne" 77). Moreover, these multifarious voices augment the ability to reach a wider audience, enhancing the essay's power and effectiveness, reflecting the freedom of the essay form. For example, within her discussion of female writers over the past centuries, Woolf's voice becomes intellectually authoritative, assertive in its pronouncements about the writing life. After discussing Mrs. Behn, she clearly states that "masterpieces are not single and solitary births; they are the outcome of many years of thinking in common, of thinking by the body of the people, so that the experience of the mass is behind the single voice" (65), a statement allusive of T. S. Eliot's comments regarding literary tradition. Later, this intellectual voice comments on novel writing.

> If one shuts one's eyes and thinks of the novel as a whole, it
> would seem to be a creation owning a certain looking-glass

likeness to life, though of course with simplifications and
distortions innumerable. At any rate, it is a structure leaving
a shape on the mind's eye, built now in squares, now pagoda
shaped, now throwing out wings and arcades, now solidly
compact and domed like the Cathedral of Saint Sofia at
Constantinople. (71)

Even though this voice seems almost academic, her use of anaphora
allows the prose to reflect the cadence of a poet: "now in squares,
now pagoda...now throwing...now solidly...." Once again, Woolf's
stylistic combinations demonstrate her interest in creating new forms,
pushing and expanding the definition and possibility of the essay
tradition. Woolf herself explains that one must "devise some entirely
new combination of her resources...so as to absorb the new into the old
without disturbing the infinitely intricate and elaborate balance of the
whole" (qtd. in Jones 234). Here Woolf demonstrates that her interest
primarily centers on form and ideas rather than on polemic, as so many
critics would have readers believe.

Along with this intellectual voice, Woolf employs a candid,
uninhibited voice as she does when propounding her thoughts on the
female gender.

Women are supposed to be very calm generally: but women
feel just as men feel; they need exercise for their faculties and a

> field for their efforts as much as their brothers do; they suffer
> from too rigid a restraint, too absolute a stagnation, precisely
> as men would suffer; and it is narrow-minded in their more
> privileged fellow-creatures to say that they ought to confine
> themselves to make puddings and knitting stockings, to
> playing on the piano and embroidering bags. (69)

As aggressive as this voice becomes, she later employs a voice even more confrontational: "I refuse to allow you, Beadle though you are, to turn me off the grass. Lock up your libraries if you like; but there is no gate, no, no bolt that you can set upon the freedom of my mind"(76). Her boldness here contrasts with the unassertive and tentative voice that opens the essay: "I soon saw that it had one fatal drawback. I should never be able to come to a conclusion. I should never be able to fulfill what is, I understand, the first duty of a lecturer"(3). Even the contrast in diction illuminates Woolf's disparate voices, her flexibility to manipulate syntax, the latter comments beginning quickly with an active transitive verb ("refuse") catapulting toward its object ("you, Beadle"); the former containing diction of failure ("fatal," "should never"), and of weakness (powerless verbs—"should be able", "is"). Even the more active syntax—"I understand"—is syntactically made weak by its placement as a parenthetical interrupter. The contrast between these two demonstrates the versatile options available to the essayist. Moreover, the variety in voice adds a protean quality to

Woolf's portrait of a female artist, a useful trait for the writer hoping to avoid the potentially narrow appropriation of critics.

In between these antithetical voices lie others. For instance, one voice employs humor. When Woolf prepares to disclose the original and provocative content of Mary Carmichael's novel, she first stops and asks, "Are there no men present? Do you promise me that behind that red curtain over there the figure of Sir Chartres Biron is not concealed? We are all women, you assure me? Then I may tell you ..."(82). In this passage, Zwerdling discusses how Woolf's use of humor regarding "Chloe" has introduced "an important human tie neglected in previous fiction"—the relationship between women—and has "said it without proclaiming it and by playing down its more controversial aspects" (256). Once again, the flexibility of the essay form, along with Woolf's use of voice, provides an opportunity to present volatile topics that distance herself—and allow the audience, too, to distance themselves—from the topic as well. Though not every audience member might embrace her topic, each may not completely close himself from it.

Still another voice is one of mentor, as perhaps mother, and as perhaps the traditional explicit essayist, as Woolf expresses the hope that Mary Carmichael does not

see the bishops and the deans, the doctors and the professors,

the patriarchs and the pedagogues all at her shouting warning
and advice. You can't do this and you shan't do that....
Aspiring and graceful female novelists this way! So they kept
at her like the crowd at a fence on the race-course, and it was
her trial to take her fence without looking to right or left. If
you stop to curse you are lost, I said to her; equally if you stop
to laugh. Hesitate or fumble and you are done for. Think
only of the jump, I implored her, as if I had put the whole of
my money on her back; and she went over it like a bird. But
there was a fence beyond that and a fence beyond that. (93-94)

Interestingly, Woolf's voice may be read as anticipating criticism
against her expansion of the essay form—"you shan't do that." Woolf
has, however, jumped the fence—the limited traditional form of the
essay has traveled beyond the narrow vision of what the essay can
accomplish. Woolf's desire to see beyond these fences, and to urge
her audience to do so as well, occurs in her letters, too. In a letter to
Dorothy Brett, dated 1930, Woolf thanks Brett for her praise of *A Room
of One's Own*. Woolf then admits, "I wanted them [the young women
scholars] to swallow certain ideas with a view to setting their brains to
work" (Letters IV 167). Woolf wishes her audience to work not merely
on the surface of her essay—the topic of women and fiction in relation
to male tradition, a topic upon which modern academics have focused
their passionate intensities—but below this surface, below the veneer

where genuine experimentation takes place, where lies Woolf's larger concern for form and freedom.

Once more, as elsewhere, these expository voices contain the freedom of poetic imagery—as with the image of "the fence"—or the domestic imagery of clothing, such as in her explanation of what the female writer ought to choose as her topic. Poetic language is, of course, not limited to the descriptive mode, but that it appears in exposition startles and jostles those who wish to appropriate even Woolf's exposition.

> There are so many new facts for her to observe. She will not need to limit herself any longer to the respectable houses of the upper middle classes. She will go without kindness or condescension, but in the spirit of fellowship into those small, scented rooms where sit the courtesan, the harlot and the lady with the pug dog. There they still sit in the rough and ready-made clothes that the male writer has had perforce to clap upon their shoulders. But Mary Carmichael will have out her scissors and fit them close to every hollow and angle (88).

These comments relate not simply to the content of what young writers should choose as their subjects, but they speak of the essay form itself— it will "not limit."

Moreover, her choice of clothing as a primary image reinforces the thought that the lives of women contain a rich supply of intellectual possibilities. The domestic image as well represents another analogue for the essay, the endless possibilities within the ordinary world.

Feminist critics, however, see this imagery in political terms. Joplin, for instance, believes that Woolf's domestic images now become a powerful and subversive force against traditional male images (4). In addition, Julie Solomon recognizes the domestic image of a room as

> a potent political metaphor for women because it concretizes visually, tactilely, the politicization of the personal and the personalization of the political. The achieving of personal space in *A Room of One's Own*, as opposed to a simple place within someone else's framework, makes woman into respected citizen, constitutes her as a political subject. (332)

Echoing Solomon's observations is Squier, who believes that Woolf's use of domestic images are "ideal subjects for the modern woman writer because the reality they embody has been passed over by literary tradition. Woolf's attention to them...typifies the revisionist impulse characteristic of her mature writing" (7).

Finally, Woolf produces the voice of the satirist. This voice occurs in her peroration to her audience:

> ...you are, in my opinion, disgracefully ignorant. You have

> never made a discovery of any sort of importance. You have
> never shaken an empire or led an army into battle. The plays
> of Shakespeare are not by you, and you have never introduced
> a barbarous race to the blessings of civilization. What is your
> excuse? (112)

Adopting and anticipating the voices of entrapment, of restriction,
specifically those scholars who will too quickly make unreasonable
demands on women and will evaluate their progress and performance
unrealistically, here Woolf, as throughout the essay, seeks to prepare
her audience to confront intellectual discrimination. Her feigned
admonition warns her audience of criticisms they might encounter.

> When you reflect upon these immense privileges and the
> length of time during which they have been enjoyed, and the
> fact that there must be at this moment some two thousand
> women capable of earning over five hundred a year in one
> way or another, you will agree that the excuse of lack of
> opportunity, training, encouragement, leisure and money no
> longer holds good. Moreover, the economists are telling us
> that Mrs. Seton has had too many children. (113)

This emphasis on "two thousand women capable..." and living in
a world where the old paradigm "no longer holds good" reflect the
opportunity which is at the pulse of genuine freedom.

These voices of mentor, mother, and satirist all point to Woolf's desire to present herself as a model before her audience, a teacher who wishes to inspire action. And the essay form itself is teacher. It is experiment, it is risk. Several critics recognize this impulse in Woolf's essay. Lillian Bisson sees Woolf as a teacher,

> modeling good teaching behaviors [that consist] of her assuming the role in which students often find themselves when facing a difficult assignment and then showing them how to move from initial helplessness to self-assured command. (202)

Vara Neverow examines Woolf's essay similarly, commenting that Woolf

> illustrates constructive critical response through the narrator's appraisal of Mary Carmichael's novel, demonstrating that the ways teachers read students' work need not parallel the ways that patriarchal critics read women writers' work. (62)

Jane Marcus, however, returns to the feminist appropriation, insisting that Woolf's tone is more aggressive than merely pedagogic, suggesting that Woolf wishes "the recruitment and enlistment of a new generation of women in the cause of feminist scholarship" (176). Marcus does Woolf a disservice because her aggressive call only serves to shelve Woolf's work into a corner bookshelf; it is a request that limits the possibilities for reading Woolf that she herself as an essayist worked so arduously to develop. Marcus's call achieves the opposite of what Woolf so much appreciates in the essayist—in this case De Quincey: "Our minds, thus widened and lulled to a width of apprehension, stand open to receive one by one in slow and stately procession the ideas which De Quincey wishes us to receive; the gold fullness of life..." ("De Quincey's Autobiography" 142).

Chapter Five
PERSUASION

Finally, Woolf provides examples of persuasion, specific appeals to reason (*logos*). Demonstrating that the traditional essay is not without merit, that the traditional still has its function, her point about the essay form is expansion, not deletion, that tradition has a place, a purpose, which can only be enhanced in the context of a more multifarious essay style. Though, as mentioned previously, several passages of exposition and description develop *ethos* and *pathos* in support of her overall argument, Woolf employs the traditional syllogism and uses Aristotle's topics. First, Woolf borrows from Aristotle's topics to generate material for her appeal to reason, arguing by degree and arguing from authoritative testimony. For instance, she reasons by degree when asserting the extraordinary odds women face as writers. She first establishes the arduousness of the writing life, that it is "almost always a feat of prodigious difficulty. Everything is against the likelihood that it will come from the writer's mind whole and entire"(51). Moreover, Woolf explains, society does not provide encouragement, for it "does not care whether Flaubert finds the right word or whether Carlyle scrupulously verifies this or that fact" (52). This lack of encouragement only frustrates the creative process, causing great poets to sing, "mighty poets in their misery dead," Woolf writes.

At this point, Woolf has demonstrated the obstacles of producing intellectual art. Next, she asks her audience to evaluate the increased degree of difficulty to which women must write, a challenge "infinitely more formidable" (52), she explains. After reminding her audience of the monetary obstacles, she speaks of the psychological obstacles, remarking that the "indifference of the world which Keats and Flaubert and other men of genius have found so hard to bear was in her case not indifference but hostility"(52). Furthermore, in case her audience has forgotten the reality of the visceral criticism toward women, Woolf quickly quotes from authoritative testimony, citing professor Brown's evaluation of his examinations and Mr. Greg of the *Saturday Review*, who states, "the essentials of a woman's being are that they are supported by, and they minister to, men"(54).

Woolf continues to use testimony to support her argument that female artists require financial independence. Sir Arthur Quillen-Couch, for instance. who verifies that intellectual genius is dependent upon economic resources.

> "What are the great poetical names of the last hundred years or so?...of these, all but Keats, Browning, Rossetti were University men; and of these three, Keats, who died young, cut off in his prime, was the only one not fairly well to do. It may seem a brutal thing to say, and it is a sad thing to say: but, as a matter of hard fact, the theory that poetical genius bloweth where it listeth, and equally in poor and rich, holds little truth...the poor poet has not in these days, nor has had for two hundred

years, a dog's chance." (107)

This authoritative testimony, made perhaps more convincing and acceptable because it is from the male world, provides the premise for Woolf's second method for appealing to reason—the syllogism, her first premises drawn from all of history.

> That is it. Intellectual freedom depends upon material things. Poetry depends upon intellectual freedom. And women have always been poor, not for two hundred years merely, but from the beginning of time. Women have had less intellectual freedom than the sons of Athenian slaves. (108)

What Woolf creates here, according to Jones, is the traditional syllogism. Jones outlines the following:

> Major premise: Intellectual freedom requires wealth.
> Minor premise: Poetry requires intellectual freedom.
> Conclusion: Art requires wealth. (230)

Jones further explains that Woolf expects her audience to apply this to women: "Because women are poor, they have no intellectual freedom and, consequently, cannot create art"(230).

Woolf's use of classical reason demonstrates that her expansion of the essay form is not a movement toward exclusion. Nor is her attitude as essayist one who seeks complete departure from what has occurred within the form of the essay. By incorporating, often reshaping traditional essay strategy, Woolf produces a timeless form, one not bound by the past, nor bound in the present moment, but one fluid in time.

Chapter Six
FINAL THOUGHTS

A Room of One's Own deserves a discussion that appreciates Woolf's essay in its totality—both its form and its content. A discussion that merely focuses on content and the political ramifications of such is incomplete and fails to elucidate the genuine sense of freedom that Woolf so often spoke—both freedom for the female artist and freedom for the essay genre. Moreover, a more complete discussion of the essay's form and its relationship to its content can amplify and strengthen the feminist discussion. The pulse of freedom and opportunity does not merely beat within the content of *A Room of One's Own*; the pulse of freedom and opportunity beats within the form itself. This unification of form and content is what imitates the highest expression of freedom.

Throughout the essay, Woolf recognizes that she stands at a liminal point, a threshold on which she can expand the creative vision of the essay form, a form possible of the greatest liberty. At this liminal moment where before her audience lies enormous potential, Woolf believes she can effect change—not merely change in the role of the female artist, as the surface topic of the essay speaks, but change in the essay form. While she comments that currently "there is no mark on the wall to measure the precise height of women" (85), there is equally no mark on the wall to measure the potential of the essay form. And as "Few women even now have been graded at the universities; the great trials of the professions, army and navy, trade, politics and diplomacy have hardly tested them" (86), so the literary world is now only beginning to test and to experiment with the essay. These are comments of opportunity, of limitless freedom, comments that seek "a liberation and wholeness of self. It is a brilliant and graceful protest against any narrower, more abstract, or merely professional critical purpose" (361), as Barbara Currier Bell and Carol Ohmann assert. In other words, Woolf wishes to mark the wall herself. When one finishes reading her final comments, one is certain that she has indeed marked the wall well.

WORKS CITED

Bell, Barbara Currier and Carol Ohmann. "Virginia Woolf's
    Criticism: A Polemical Preface." *Critical Inquiry* 1 (1974): 361-71.

Bennett, Arnold. "Queen of the High-Brows." [Rev. of A Room of
    One's Own.] *Evening Standard* 28 Nov. 1929: 9. Rpt in
    Virginia Woolf: The Criticial Heritage. Ed. Robin Majumdar
    and Allen McLaurin. London: Routledge & Kegan Paul, 1975.
    258-260.

Bisson, Lillian M. "Doodling Her Way to Insight: From
    Incompetent Student to Empowered Rhetor in *A Room of One's Own.*"
    *Virginia Woolf: Emerging Perspectives Selected Papers from the Third Annual
    Conference on Virginia Woolf.* Ed. Mark Hussey and Vara Neverow. New
    York: Pace University Press, 1994.

Burt, John. "Irreconcilable Habits of Thought in *A Room of One's
    Own* and *To the Lighthouse.*" *ELH* 49.4 (Winter 1982): 889-907.

Caughie, Pamela L. *Virginia Woolf & Postmodernism: Literature
    in Quest & Question of Itself.* Chicago: University of Illinois Press, 1991.

Corbett, Edward P.J. and Robert J. Connors. *Classical Rhetoric
    for the Modern Student.* Fourth edition. New York: Oxford
    University Press, 1999.

Farrell, Thomas J. "The Female and Male Modes of Rhetoric."
    College English 40(April 1979):909-921.

Fernald, Anne. "*A Room of One's Own*, Personal Criticism, and
    the Essay." *Twentieth Century Literature.* 40.2 (Summer 1994): 165-189.

Gualtieri, Elena. *Virginia Woolf's Essays: Sketching the Past.*

New York: St. Martin's Press, 2000.

Hoban, James L. "Rhetorical *Topoi* in *A Room of One's Own*." In
    RE: Reading, RE: Writing, RE: Teaching: Selected Papers
    from the Fourth Annual Conference on Virginia Woolf. Eds.
    Eileen Barrett and Patricia Cramer. New York: Pace
    University Press, 1995. 148-154.

Hynes, Nancy. "The Chamelon Voice and Classical Structure in
    Three Guineas and *A Room of One's Own*." *Virginia Woolf: Emerging*
    Perspectives Selected Papers from the Third Annual Conference on Virginia
    Woolf. Eds. Mark Hussey and Vara Neverow. New York: Pace University
    Press, 1994. 140-146.

Jones, Ellen Carol. "Androgynous Vision and Artistic Process in
    Virginia Woolf's *A Room of One's Own*." In *Critical Essays on Virginia*
    Woolf. Ed. Morris Beja. MA: G.K.Hall & Co., 1985. 227-239.

Joplin, Patricia. "'I Have Bought My Freedom': *The Gift of A*
    Room of One's Own." *Virginia Woolf Miscellany*. 21 (Fall 1983):4-5.

Lee, Hermione. "Virginia Woolf's Essays." In *The Cambridge*
    Companion to Virginia Woolf. Eds. Sue Roe and Susan Sellers. Cambridge:
    Cambridge University Press, 2000. 91-108.

Long, Jean. "The Awkward Break: Woolf's Reading of Brontee and
    Austen in A Room of One's Own." *Woolf Studies Annual*. 3 (1997): 76-94.

Lukacs, Gyorgy. *Soul and Form*. Trans. Anna Bostcok. MA: MIT
    Press, 1971.

Marchi, Dudley M. "Virginia Woolf Crossing the Borders of
    History, Culture, and Gender: The Case of Montaigne, Pater, and
    Gournay." *Comparative Literature Studies*. 34 (1997):1-31.

Marcus, Jane. "Sapphistry: Narration as Lesbian Seduction in *A Room of One's Own." Virginia Woolf and the Languages of Patriarchy*. Indianapolis: Indiana University Press, 1987. 163-188.

Marcus, Jane. "'Taking the Bull by the Udders': Sexual Difference in Virginia Woolf—a Conspiracy Theory." *In Virginia Woolf and Bloomsbury*. Ed. Jane Marcus. Bloomington, Indiana: Indiana University Press, 1987. 146-169.

Marcus, Jane. "Still Practice, A/Wrested Alphabet: Toward a Feminist Aesthetic." *Tulsa Studies in Women's Literature*. 3 (1984):79-97.

Marcus, Laura. "Woolf's Feminism and Feminism's Woolf." In *The Cambridge Companion to Virginia Woolf*. Eds. Sue Roe and Susan Sellers. Cambridge: Cambridge University Press, 2000. 209-244.

Naremore, James. *The World Without a Self*. New Haven: Yale University Press, 1973.

Neverow, Vara. "*A Room of One's Own* as a Model of Composition Theory." In *Virginia Woolf: Emerging Perspectives Selected Papers from the Third Annual Conference on Virginia Woolf*. Ed. Mark Hussey and Vara Neverow. New York: Pace University Press, 1994. 58-64.

Rogat, Ellen Hawkes. "A Form of One's Own." *Mosaic*. 8 (1974): 77-90.

Rosenman, Ellen Bayuk. *A Room of One's Own: Women Writers and the Politics of Creativity*. New York: Twayne, 1995.

Rosenthal, Michael. "Social Criticism: *A Room of One's Own* and *Three Guineas." Virginia Woolf*. New York: Columbia UP, 1979. 218-243.

Rusk, Lauren. "Woolf and Empire in *A Room of One's Own*." *Virginia Woolf Miscellany*. 47 (Spring 1996): 4.

Solomon, Julie Robin. "Staking Ground: the Politics of Space in
    Virginia Woolf's *A Room of One's Own and Three Guineas." Women's
    Studies: An Interdisciplinary Journal.* 16(1989): 331-347.

Squier, Susan M. *Virginia Woolf and London: The Sexual
    Politics of the City.* Chapel Hill: University of North Carolina Press, 1985.

Squier, Susan. "Mirroring and Mothering: Reflections on the
    Mirror Encounter Metaphor in Virginia Woolf's Works." *Twentieth
    Century Literature.* 27 (1981): 272-288.

Zwerdling, Alex. "Anger and Conciliation in *A Room of One's Own
    and Three Guineas." Virginia Woolf and the Real World.* Los Angeles:
    University of California Press, 1986. 243-270.

Woolf, Virginia. *A Change of Perspective: The Letters of
    Virginia Woolf. Volume III*: 1923-1928. Ed. Nigel Nicolson. London:
    Hogarth Press, 1977.

Woolf, Virginia. "De Quincey's Autobiography." In *The Second
    Common Reader.* New York: Harcourt Brace, 1932. 141-149.

Woolf, Virginia. "Mr. Bennett and Mrs. Brown." In *The Captain's
    Death Bed and Other Essays.* New York: Harcourt Brace Jovanovich, 1950.

Woolf, Virginia. *Congenial Spirits: The Selected Letters of
    Virginia Woolf.* Ed. Joanne Trautmann Banks. New York: Harcourt Brace
    Jovanovich, 1989.

Woolf, Virginia. "The Decay of Essay Writing." *The Essays of
    Virginia Woolf. Volume I*: 1904-1912. Ed. Andrew McNeillie. New York:
    Harcourt Brace Jovanovich, 1986. 24-27.

Woolf, Virginia. "Mr. Symon's Essays." *The Essays of Virginia*

Woolf. Volume II: 1912-1918. Ed. Andrew McNeillie. New York:
Harcourt Brace Jovanovich, 1987. 67-71.

Woolf, Virginia. "A Book of Essays." *The Essays of Virginia
Woolf. Volume II: 1912-1918*. Ed. Andrew McNeillie. New York:
Harcourt Brace Jovanovich, 1987. 212-214.

Woolf, Virginia. "Imitative Essays." *The Essays of Virginia
Woolf. Volume II: 1912-1918*. Ed. Andrew McNeillie. New York:
Harcourt Brace Jovanovich, 1987. 248-249.

Woolf, Virginia. "Bad Writers." *The Essays of Virginia
Woolf. Volume II: 1912-1918*. Ed. Andrew McNeillie. New York:
Harcourt Brace Jovanovich, 1987. 326-329.

Woolf, Virginia. "Montaigne." *The Essays of Virginia Woolf.
Volume IV: 1919-1929*. Ed. Andrew McNeillie. New York: Harcourt
Brace Jovanovich, 1988. 71-81.

Woolf, Virginia. "The Modern Essay." *The Essays of Virginia
Woolf. Volume IV: 1919-1929*. Ed. Andrew McNeillie. New York:
Harcourt Brace Jovanovich, 1988. 215-224.

Woolf, Virginia. *A Reflection of the other Person: The Letters
of Virginia Woolf. Volume IV: 1929-1931*. Ed. Andrew McNeillie.
London: Hogarth, 1994.

Woolf, Virginia. "Impassioned Prose." *The Essays of Virginia
Woolf. Volume IV: 1919-1929*. Ed. Andrew McNeillie. New York:
Harcourt Brace Jovanovich, 1988. 361-370.

Woolf, Virginia. *A Room of One's Own*. New York: Harcourt Brace
& Company, 1989.

[Unsigned review, *Times Literary Supplement*] 8 October 1931.

773   Rpt *in Virginia Woolf: The Criticial Heritage*. Ed.
Robin Majumdar and Allen McLaurin. London: Routledge &
Kegan Paul, 1975.

V.Sackville-West. [rev. of *A Room of One's Own*] *Listener* 6
    November 1929.620 Rpt *in Virginia Woolf: The Criticial
    Heritage*. Ed. Robin Majumdar and Allen McLaurin. London:
    Routledge & Kegan Paul, 1975.

WORKS CONSULTED

Batchelor, J.B. "Feminism in Virginia Woolf." *English*. 17 (Spring 1968):1-7.

Bowlby, Rachel. "The Trained Mind: *A Room of One's Own.*"
Virginia Woolf: Feminist Destinations. Oxford: Basil Blackwell, 1988. Rpt
in Virginia Woolf: A Collection of Critical Essays. Ed. Margaret Homans.
NJ: Prentice Hall, 1993. 174-195

Colburn, Krystyna. "Women's Oral Tradition and *A Room of One's
Own.*" *RE: Reading, RE: Writing, RE: Teaching: Selected Papers from the
Fourth Annual Conference on Virginia Woolf*. Eds. Eileen Barrett and
Patricia Cramer. New York: Pace University Press, 1995.

Cuddy-Keane, Melba. "Opening Historical Doors to the Room: An
Approach to Teaching." *RE: Reading, RE: Writing, RE: Teaching: Selected
Papers from the Fourth Annual Conference on Virginia Woolf*. Eds. Eileen
Barrett and Patricia Cramer. New York: Pace University Press, 1995.

Ezell, Margaret J.M. "The Myth of Judith Shakespeare: Creating
the Canon of Women's Literature." *ELH*. 21.3 (Spring 1990):579-592.

Folsom, Marcia McClintock. "Gallant Red Brick and Plain China:
Teaching *A Room of One's Own.*" *College English*. 45 (1983): 254-62.

Fox, Alice. "Literary Allusion as Feminist Criticism in *A Room
of One's Own.*" Philological Quarterly. 63 (1984):145-162.

Gorsky, Susan Rubinow. *Virginia Woolf*. Revised Edition.
Boston: Twayne, 1989.

Greene, Sally. "Hidden Persuasion in *A Room of One's Own.*"
Virginia Woolf Miscellany. 46 (1995 Fall): 5-6.

Kaivola, Karen. "Revisiting Woolf's Representations of
Androgyny." *Tulsa Studies in Women's Literature*. 18 (1999 Fall):235-261

Laroche, Rebecca. "Laura at the Crossroads: *A Room of One's Own* and the Elizabethan Sonnet." In *Virginia Woolf: Reading the Renaissance*. Ed. Sally Greene. Athens, Ohio: Ohio UP, 1999. 192-210.

Marchi, Dudley M. "Virginia Woolf Crossing the Borders of History, Culture, and Gender: The Case of Montaigne, Pater, and Gournay." *Comparative Literature Studies*. 34 (1997):1-31.

Marcus, Jane. "Quentin's Bogey." *Critical Inquiry*. 11 (March 1985): 486-497.

McGill, Allyson F. "Re: Teaching: Woolf and Vera Brittain; Marina Tsvetaeva." *RE: Reading, RE: Writing, RE: Teaching: Selected Papers from the Fourth Annual Conference on Virginia Woolf*. Eds. Eileen Barrett and Patricia Cramer. New York: Pace University Press, 1995.

Miller, Casey and Kate Swift. *Words and Women*. NY: Doubleday, 1976.

Pacey, Desmond. "Virginia Woolf as a Literary Critic." *University of Toronto Quarterly*. 28 (April 1948):234-44.

Pelham Edgar. *The Art of the Novel from 1700 to the Present Time*. Macmillan, 1933.

Richter, Harvena. "Virginia Woolf and Mary Hamilton." *Virginia Woolf Miscellany*. 24 (Spring 1985):1.

Roe, Sue. "Floundering: *A Room of One's Own.*" *Writing and Gender: Virginia Woolf's Writing Practice*. New York: St. Martin's Press, 1990. 81-91.

Rosenbaum, S.P. "The Manuscript Versions of *A Room of One's Own.*" *Virginia Woolf Miscellany*. 38 (Spring 1992): 4.

Schwartz, Beth C. "Thinking Back through Our Mothers: Virginia Woolf Reads Shakespeare." *ELH*. 58: 721-46. (1991)

West, Rebecca. "Autumn and Virginia Woolf" *In Ending in Earnest:*

A Literary Log. Doubleday, Doran, 1931. 208-213.

Winterhalter, Teresa. "Guns and Big Guns in *A Room of One's Own." RE: Reading, RE: Writing, RE: Teaching: Selected Papers from the Fourth Annual Conference on Virginia Woolf.* Eds. Eileen Barrett and Patricia Cramer. New York: Pace University Press, 1995.

Wyndham Lewis. "Virginia Woolf ('Mind' and 'Matter' on the Plane of a Literary Controversy)," In *Men without Art.* Russels & Russell, 1964. 158-71

Zimmerman, Dorothy. "Woolf as Feminist." *Prairie Schooner.* (Summer 1971):173-174.

ACKNOWLEDGMENTS

Excerpts from *A Room of One's Own* by Virginia Woolf. Copyright 1929 by Houghton Mifflin Harcourt Publishing Company. Copyright (c) Renewed 1957 by Leonard Woolf. Reprinted by permission of Houghton Mifflin Harcourt Publishing Company. All rights reserved.

Cover art, "Sepia Writing Desk." Copyright 2010 by Manuel Velasco. Licensed by istockphoto LP, Alberta, Canada.